ME

MYSELF

AND I

BODY CHANGES

Published in Great Britain 2019
dftakecontrol

ISBN: 978-0-9569771-9-9

© Copyright text Dr Funke Baffour 2019

Acknowledgments

I am grateful to God for everything I am able to do and indeed learn. Working with young people has been the highlight of my career. I therefore dedicate this book to all the young people who have shared their stories with me. You have all inspired me to dig deep and to continue to do so!

I would like to thank my husband and children for the joy they bring to my life.

I would like to thank my siblings for their continuous support.

I would also like to thank Matilda for her assistance with this book.

I would like to thank Dr Fatma Odaymat and Mr Titi-Ofei for enabling me to work with their students to support their emotional wellbeing.

Finally, I would like to acknowledge and thank you all for making the decision to read this book. This book may be targeted at adolescents, but it is also helpful for parents, guardians and those working with young people.

CONTENTS

4

Me, Myself and I

Hi,

I am **Dr Funke!**

Are you a teenager? Are you going through physical changes that you need guidance about? Are you going through an emotional ride of roller coasters? Are you very shy or always feeling judged? Are you afraid of talking to boys or girls? Are you being peer pressured by your friends or strangers to try something new that you are uncomfortable doing?

If you're one of these people (or all) and need some help and guidance, you've come to the right place! Welcome to my new mini-series Me, Myself and I. This series was created for young people like you to help you understand your mind and body and the changes you are experiencing in every aspect of your life.

Each book in the series will explore some of the struggles related to a young person's identity. Identity – the fact of being who or what a person or thing is – is a complex concept. What does it mean to be you? Your genetics physically make you you, but you are in control of everything else! How you treat yourself and others, what you believe in and how you act are all your personal choices.

How do I find my identity if I can't see it?

With time.

Who can help me track down my identity?

Unfortunately, no one can. This is a mission for you and you alone. But you are lucky; you have the ability to be yourself. Do not take this for granted.

When will I know my identity?

I don't know either! Maybe in a year or maybe in a decade. Finding your identity is an ongoing hunt, requiring you to soak in as much of the world around you as you can.

Sometimes we can lose who we are. We are not sure why we make the choices we do or, more broadly, what our purpose here is. Knowing yourself is not something you can accomplish overnight. It takes many years and periods of reflection to understand who you are and what you are capable of.

Do not become frustrated. Instead, use the books in this series to help guide your thinking and reflection on who you are growing up to be and what, if anything, you want to change about yourself. You have the power to make decisions and live the life you want to. Do not let anyone take this away from you.

One of my main hopes is that this series excites your curiosity. I ask some tough questions that will cause you to look inward, finding the answers within yourself.

The bottom line is you are special. You are beautiful. You are loved.

Introduction

Welcome to Body Changes, the third book in the mini-series Me, Myself and I. This book was written for young people like you and aims at tackling important questions, breaking down myths about sex and puberty and giving you guidance on how to navigate the tricky life experiences you may encounter.

As a teenager, adapting to sudden changes in your body can be a difficult process. These physical, psychological and emotional changes are indicators that you're moving out of childhood and into adolescence, and this can either be very exciting or very daunting.

Did you know that having mood swings is a big part of puberty? It's true! You may suddenly feel irritated, sad or even confused by the smallest things. Don't be alarmed; it's a natural process that everyone goes through. However, we all experience puberty in different ways, and having the right facts will help you navigate this important period of your life.

Your body will go through an adjustment, whether it is a physical adjustment caused by your changing hormones or simply an adjustment in the way you think and feel. You will experience strong emotions that you have never felt before, and you may even become anxious or feel like you are the only person in the world who feels the way you do. Just keep in mind that there are 829,610,031 teenagers in the world, and each one is going through the same thing that you are (yes, I counted every single one of them. Well... not personally).

This book will give you the tools you need to help yourself during this important period of your life. We will be talking about the biology of your body, and, yes, that includes a discussion about sex. This is something you may have already touched on in your biology lesson, but this book will go a little deeper so that you are loaded with all the facts.

As a teenager, you will notice that there is a lot of talk about sex, either in the media or from your peers. While Uncle Google may be your 'go-to' for information, what you find may leave you feeling more confused than when you began. This book is here to help you become an informed thinker so that you do not fall into any potholes during your journey into adolescence.

You hold the keys to your thoughts and actions, and it's important that you hold the right keys. When you have the right facts, all you have to do is stay aligned with who you are and reflect on all that you do in a calm and confident way.

In this book, we will address issues that you may find difficult to discuss with your parents and friends, as well as experiences that will guide you on how to make informed decisions.

Throughout this book, you will find several 'reflection corners' that will present you with different stories, scenarios and questions to help you reflect on and improve your relationship with your body. At the end of the book, there are blank pages you can use to write down your notes and reflections as you work your way through each chapter and activity.

Before we get started, please complete this short questionnaire designed to help you explore the perceptions you have about yourself. Please answer as honestly as you can!

DF Body Perception Questionnaire

	Yes	Sometimes	No
1. I often forget to keep my body clean.			
2. I don't know how to keep my body safe.			
3. I worry about what other people say about my body.			
4. I spend too much time thinking about how to change parts of my body.			
5. I feel that some parts of my body are unattractive.			
6. I get upset because my body is growing slower or faster than my peers.			
7. I am dissatisfied by what I see when I look in the mirror.			
8. If I had the chance, I would change parts of my body.			
9. When other people say hurtful things about my body, I believe them.			
10. I have the desire to look like someone else.			

If the majority of your answers were 'No', this implies that you have a great relationship with your body. However, if you answered 'Yes' to one or more of these questions, you may be having some challenges with the way you view your body, or the view that others have of your body is having an unhealthy impact on you. If you answered 'sometimes' to one or more of these questions, this implies that you may be confused about how you view your body. But this can be normal, being a teenager!

Most teenagers have some confusion or hang-ups about their bodies, and that's perfectly normal. However, allowing those unhealthy thoughts to linger can have an impact on your relationship with your body. In this book, we will explore how you can improve your relationship with your body so that you are equipped to deal with any challenges you may face.

After you have finished this book, come back to this section and re-answer these questions. You may find – and I hope you will! – that your perceptions have changed after learning more about your body.

As you read through this book, take your time to reflect on each section and, especially, take notes.

Enjoy!

Changing
Bodies

Puberty

Some of you may have already been through puberty and have gone through rapid physical, mental, and emotional changes.

These changes include:

Physical body changes.

Independent thinking and making decisions for yourself.

Changes in the dynamic between you and your family – they treat you less like a child, give you more responsibilities, trust you to make your own decisions and check up on you less than they used to.

Caring more about the opinions of your friends.

Changes in your emotions – they become complicated and harder to navigate.

Facing difficult decisions and running into situations where you don't know who to turn to.

Feeling peer pressure to have a boyfriend or girlfriend.

Trying drugs or seeing drugs being used in school and your community.

Your parents being too uncomfortable or too busy to talk to you about the changes you're going through.

This list may seem overwhelming or even frightening, but these are things that some may experience during puberty.

With the knowledge laid out in this book, you will develop a better understanding of these life situations. Understanding these situations will also help you to navigate them more easily!

It is incredibly important to be aware of the experiences you may run into, whether they be good or bad. Many young people think they are invincible and that nothing bad can ever happen to them. Unfortunately, that is not true.

While it's possible to avoid bad situations, it is up to you to solve any problems you may run into, deal with the consequences and learn from the situation. Remember this mantra: **challenges are growth**. And you never have to suffer in silence.

This is a major time of growth, and with growth comes challenge and the necessity to overcome those challenges. While this may be a difficult time, growing up is a journey that you only get to experience once, so enjoy it while you can.

CHALLENGES ARE GROWTH

Body Changes

Some of you have already been through physical body changes. This usually happens during a stage called puberty, which is when you change physically, emotionally and mentally from a child into a young adult.

Five major things change during this time:

1. Height

2. Hormones

3. Genitals and private parts

4. Body hair and skin

5. Your mind

Some of you may be going through these changes, and some may not have started yet. Everyone starts developing at different times, and those development move at different paces. That's what makes you unique.

Height: The Growth Spurt

One of the most significant physical changes that occur during puberty is the 'growth spurt'. The growth spurt is when you start growing noticeably taller, and the height differences between boys and girls start to become more obvious.

Normally, girls start to grow taller around the age of ten or eleven. The growth spurt lasts around three years, and, during this time, girls are generally taller than boys of the same age.

Boys, on the other hand, start their growth spurt later at around the age of twelve or thirteen. Their growth spurts last longer than girls, and some boys don't stop growing until they're 19 or 20.

It is important to remember that the ages listed above are averages, meaning some teenagers will start growing sooner and some later. If you're growing faster than others, or if you haven't even started yet, don't worry. Everyone grows, and so will you.

During the growth spurt, it is normal to feel awkward or clumsy. Different parts of the body grow at different rates. Your hands and feet grow first, followed by the arms, legs, hips, and chest. When you find yourself tripping over your own feet, it's simply because the rest of your body hasn't caught up to your growing feet yet.

Some boys and girls grow so rapidly that their skin can't keep up. When this happens, stretch marks begin to develop. Stretch marks are light or dark lines on the skin. They may fade or get less noticeable once you get older, or they may never disappear completely.

Before you start feeling self-conscious about your clumsy feet or the lines on your body, take a minute to realise that no one has the perfect body. You have to trust in the process of your growing body and realise that we are all perfect in our perceived imperfections.

Hormones

You're probably wondering why your body is changing the way it is. Your body is constantly producing hormones, which are special chemical messengers that tell your body how and when to change and grow.

Growth hormones are when your brain releases the chemicals that tell your body to grow. Your brain also releases sex hormones. For girls, the sex hormones are produced in the ovaries, while the hormones for the boys are produced in the testicles.

These sex hormones cause shape differences in male and female bodies. Girls' hips start to grow wider and rounder, and their waists seem smaller and narrower in comparison. The sex hormones also cause their breasts to start growing.

For boys, their shoulders start to broaden, and their arms and legs become thicker and more muscular. They even experience some swelling of their breast tissue, but that goes away with time.

Hormones also influence your emotions, and you may feel intense changes in your mood during this time. One moment you could feel amazing, and the next you feel absolutely horrible. This rollercoaster of emotion is called a 'mood swing', and it can happen at any time.

The reason why you feel such strong emotions is because of the production of hormones during puberty. When the production suddenly increases, your emotions become harder to control.

However, later in life, as the production of hormones decreases again, you will feel more in control of how you feel.

Genitals' is the technical term for private parts, which are the areas of your body you keep covered with underwear.

When you were a child, your genitals were mainly used for going to the restroom. However, now that you've entered adolescence, your hormones will cause your genitals to grow.

For girls, the skin and tissue in the genital area become softer and fatter. For boys, their penis starts to lengthen and thicken; their testicles will drop and start to make sperm, which are the male reproductive cells.

Genitals will also produce new fluids during this time. Boys start producing semen, a mucus-like fluid in which sperm can swim that comes out of the penis when a boy ejaculates. Girls produce menstrual blood and vaginal fluid, which is meant to keep the vagina lubricated.

Body Hair and Skin Changes

Along with your height, hormones and genitals, your body hair and skin will also start to change during puberty. For most teenagers, their skin starts to become oilier, which can lead to pimples, a common problem amongst adolescents.

Along with oilier and, sometimes, dryer skin, you will also start to grow hair in different areas of your body, such as on your legs and arms. Additionally, boys grow hair on their private parts, face, chest and armpits. Girls grow hair on their private parts and armpits.

The newly grown hair on your private parts is called 'pubic hair'. Some people will have a lot while others have just a little. Pubic hair serves many purposes, such as keeping your private parts clean. This is extremely important because the skin in those areas is delicate and can get easily irritated. Another purpose of your pubic hair is to help hold sweat and other secretions away from the sensitive skin of your private parts. Even though people may tease you for it, pubic hair is completely normal.

Hair growth underneath your armpits generally comes later during puberty. Many girls do not grow underarm hair until after their breasts have started to develop and after their menstrual cycles have started. Boys tend to start growing armpit hair around a year after their pubic hair has started to grow.

Facial hair is usually the last type of body hair to appear on boys. For most boys, facial hair starts growing between the ages of fifteen and eighteen, but it may start earlier or later.

Acne

It's not unusual to have a pimple or two as a teenager. However, some of you may wake up and feel like, all of a sudden, your face has been invaded by a mass of spots.

What is this, and why does it happen? Acne is the umbrella term for breakouts on the skin. When pimples start to appear on the face, back, neck and shoulders, it is because of hormonal changes. Don't worry, though; this phase often passes after puberty.

Acne can appear in one of the following ways:

1. **Blackheads**: These little, black spots are not dirt on your skin. They are bacteria or dead skin cells that have been trapped in your pores.

2. **Whiteheads**: When your pores are clogged with oil, you can get whiteheads, which are much the same as blackheads. However, whereas a blackhead is an open pore, a whitehead is a pore that has been covered by a layer of skin, trapping the bacteria and dead skin cells in the pore.

3. **Papules, pustules or nodules**: A papule is a type of inflamed blemish, also known as a pimple or zit. They develop when the hair follicle (pore) becomes clogged with skin cells and excess oil. If left untreated, a papule can become a pustule or even a nodule, which are more severe forms of papules.

   Inflammation or infections around the clogged follicle can cause pressure of the follicle walls. When the walls rapture, the bacteria spill out into the surrounding skin, causing the skin to become red, inflamed, and sore.

4. **Cysts**: Cystic acne occurs when the infection around the hair follicle goes deep into your skin. These deep, pus-filled pimples can be painful, and, if it bursts, the infection can spread, causing more breakouts. Cystic acne can appear in your teens and early 20s. The cause of these cysts is not entirely known, but they have been linked to the hormone androgens.

Unfortunately, androgens increase when you are a teenager, putting you at higher risk for cysts. Luckily, cystic acne is rare and easily treatable.

Reflection Corner

Do you think diet helps manage acne?

Do you think acne is caused by uncleanliness?

Why do some people get acne and others don't?

Reflect on these questions and devise a list of myths and truth about acne and discuss with your friends and family.

Your Mind

Your mental capacities are going to start developing during this time, as well as your critical and independent thinking skills. As a result of these cognitive changes, you will start to develop your own identity, start to think for yourself and start making your own decisions.

You will begin to perceive yourself as a unique individual, and you will even start to question everyone's opinions, thoughts and perceptions, including those of your parents, friends and even your teachers.

You may also want to experience life first-hand, rather than simply relying on what others have told you. This means you'll want to try new things and take risks.

All these mental changes are signs that you're maturing into a young adult. However, that does not mean you are actually an adult yet. You're starting to figure out life for yourself, but there are still many things you need to learn.

Therefore, it is important to know where and from whom you're getting your information. Do not be afraid to ask questions and explore! Don't assume that you have all the answers. Take this time to learn everything you can so that you can be an informed adult in the future.

Reflection Corner

Ben, a 15-year-old, wants to get a tattoo on his arm because his best friend got one. He announces his decision to his parents. Shocked, they tell him that they are against his decision as they believe that he is too young. Ignoring his parent's wishes, he decides to go ahead and get a tattoo where he can easily hide it with his clothes.

What are your views about Ben's decision? Do you think he got the tattoo because he really wanted it, or was he just taking a risk? Do you agree with his parents that he was too young to make this decision?

In this section, we're going to go over some of the specific changes that boys and girls will experience during puberty. While they may seem weird or even scary, just keep in mind that everyone is going through this process, so there's no need to feel embarrassed!

Hey Boys!

During this process, your body will start to transition from that of a boy to that of a man, and your voice will deepen due to a hormone called testosterone. It may squeak or crack while you are talking, but do not worry; this will go away soon.

Along with the other physical changes, your penis will change in shape and size,

want to try new things and take risks.

All these mental changes are signs that you're maturing into a young adult. However, that does not mean you are actually an adult yet. You're starting to figure out life for yourself, but there are still many things you need to learn.

Therefore, it is important to know where and from whom you're getting your information. Do not be afraid to ask questions and explore! Don't assume that you have all the answers. Take this time to learn everything you can so that you can be an informed adult in the future.

Reflection Corner

Ben, a 15-year-old, wants to get a tattoo on his arm because his best friend got one. He announces his decision to his parents. Shocked, they tell him that they are against his decision as they believe that he is too young. Ignoring his parent's wishes, he decides to go ahead and get a tattoo where he can easily hide it with his clothes.

What are your views about Ben's decision? Do you think he got the tattoo because he really wanted it, or was he just taking a risk? Do you agree with his parents that he was too young to make this decision?

In this section, we're going to go over some of the specific changes that boys and girls will experience during puberty. While they may seem weird or even scary, just keep in mind that everyone is going through this process, so there's no need to feel embarrassed!

Hey Boys!

During this process, your body will start to transition from that of a boy to that of a man, and your voice will deepen due to a hormone called testosterone. It may squeak or crack while you are talking, but do not worry; this will go away soon.

Along with the other physical changes, your penis will change in shape and size,

and this is something that many teenage boys worry about. You may have heard that having a small penis makes you abnormal and that you will not be able to have sex later in life. It is important to keep in mind that sexual performance is not based on the shape or size of your penis, but, instead, on the feelings that you and your partner have for one another.

Hanging below your penis is the scrotum, a sack of skin that holds the testicles. During puberty, your scrotum will start to get looser and hang lower, and your testicles will start to produce sperm.

Your penis is normally soft and hangs downward. When it is erect, however, more blood flows in and out, and the penis becomes larger, harder and stands out from the body. Many things can cause an erection, such as excitement from a sexual thought, seeing someone you find attractive, or being touched in a sexual way. Having an erection does not always mean that you need to have sex. If you wait a few minutes, your erection will go down on its own without causing any harm.

Erections happen all the time, and, sometimes, you may even have one in public. Don't worry, though! You are usually the only person who is aware of it, and it is part of the natural process of getting older.

When you have an erection, you may notice a milky, sticky fluid coming out of your penis. This happens when a man 'ejaculates' during the climax of sexual arousal.

This fluid consists of sperm, the male reproductive cell, and semen, which keeps the sperm alive. Each ejaculation, although it is only a teaspoon of liquid, contains 500 million sperm cell, and each sperm can make a female pregnant. Does that mean a female can get pregnant 500 million times? Absolutely not! The key point here is that, while the human body has some amazing abilities, there are also consequences to making uninformed decisions.

On a final note, you may have 'wet dreams' where you ejaculate in your sleep. These occur when you dream about something sexual. Not every boy has wet dreams, but most do, so do not let your friends tease you when it happens!

Hey Girls!

Just like the boys will experience some body changes, your breasts will start growing due to the hormone called 'oestrogen'. This hormone allows women to produce milk and feed their babies when they give birth later in life.

Some girls may start to develop breasts around age 8, but other girls start later. For some girls, it may take less than a year for your breasts to develop fully. For others, it can take up to six years. Please be patient!

As your breasts and nipples start developing, they may feel sore or sensitive. Cold weather or physical touch may even make your nipples momentarily hard. Don't panic; this is all normal!

Every woman's breasts look different; there is no reason to feel embarrassed about yours. Some girls may feel more comfortable wearing a bra. Whatever you feel up to doing is completely fine!

During puberty, the walls of the vagina produce a thick, sticky fluid called 'discharge'. This fluid keeps the vagina clean and maintains the proper environment for good bacteria growth. Discharge occurs during different times of the month, as well as when a female feels sexually aroused.

If your discharge becomes thick, appears yellow, green or brown or causes itching in the private parts, you may have an infection. While it's probably not serious, you should still see your doctor to make sure everything is okay.

The area around the opening of the vagina is called the 'vulva'. The opening of the vagina is normally closed and is protected by the 'labia majora' and the 'labia minora', which are the outer and inner 'lips'. These lips are two folds of skin which have many small glands where you perspire.

In front of the urethra, where the inner lips join, is the 'clitoris', a small bump of flesh about the size of a small pea. The clitoris is filled with nerve endings and is the most sensitive part of the female genitals.

Most girls begin having menstrual periods between the ages of ten and sixteen. Once puberty sets in, a girl has the possibility of becoming pregnant if she has sexual intercourse with a male. It should be noted that, whether the sexual contact was consensual or not, a girl can still become pregnant. This is something we will discuss in later chapters.

During puberty, your ovaries, which are two egg-shaped organs, start to mature and release an egg (or ovum) each month. During this release, the uterus matures, and a soft lining begins to form in preparation to receive a fertilised egg. If it does not receive one, the lining breaks down, and blood passes out of the vagina – this is your period.

I know it has taken some explanation to get to this point, but it is important that you are given the right information so that you can become informed about your reproductive organs. This may feel a bit like a biology lesson, and it might be a good idea to have follow-up discussions with your teachers about what we have discussed. They may be surprised or even impressed with your knowledge base!

Your period may be irregular for the first year or so, but it will eventually arrive around the same time each month. This can vary from 24 to 35 days, depending on the individual. Some women bleed for seven days, while others bleed for three or four. You may experience cramping around your lower abdomen, pain in your back, sore breasts, increased mood swings and bloating right before and during the beginning of your period. If you have irregular periods, it's important to seek advice from your doctor. Irregular periods can be caused by a range of things, such as medications, exercising too much or having a very low or high body weight. Your doctor will give you advice on how to regulate your periods.

Women have four options when caring for their periods:

1. Pads, or sanitary napkins, are stuck to the underwear with a sticky strip to absorb the menstrual blood, and you should change them every two to four hours, depending on your flow.

2. Tampons are small cotton tubes that you push into the vagina. The cotton absorbs the blood before it comes out onto your underwear. Some women prefer these over pads because you cannot feel them and they limit the mess. You should change them based on your flow but never keep one inside for more than eight hours.

3. Menstrual cups are small, silicone cups that are inserted into the vagina. Like tampons, they catch the blood before it comes out, and you cannot feel them once they are in. They are reusable and should be changed as often as possible to prevent infections.

4. Period pants are another option. Yes, you heard me correctly – period pants. Before you say how gross that sounds, hear me out. Period pants are super-absorbent underwear that has multiple layers to protect against any leaks, including moisture-wicking cotton, an odour-trapping lining, an absorbent fabric, and a leak-resistant barrier. They're very easy to clean, as well. All you have to do is rinse them, toss them in a cold-water wash, and air-dry them. There are numerous brands, such as Thinx and Dear Kate. However, some brands have an exterior plastic lining to keep the underwear waterproof. These are not good for the environment, so try to use one of the other brands.

A word of caution about tampon usage: if you don't change them often enough, or if you use tampons that are too absorbent, there is a risk of severe bacterial infections or toxic shock syndrome (TSS). TSS is rare but a very dangerous illness that affects your whole body. To avoid this illness, make sure you change your tampon regularly.

Period tips!

Here are some tips to make your periods easier.

Always be prepared! Keep a calendar to track when your period is coming.

Avoid eating too much salt.

Drink plenty of water or freshly made fruit juice.

Eat foods rich in iron, like fish, liver, beans, meat, and lots of greens to make up for the loss of iron during bleeding.

Do not try to regulate your emotions. Revel in your PMS tension, read a book, watch a movie and cry about whatever is making you sad.

Some females eat whatever they want during this time. While that's completely fine, there are no hard facts supporting the idea that chocolate eases the pain you're feeling. But, if you want to eat chocolate, enjoy it! You're human, and you're hungry. Just don't overdo it.

Recap: Changes That Occur for Boys and Girls

Boys	Girls
Broader shoulders and muscle mass	**Curvier hips**
Your body may have already gone through drastic changes or is still in the process of changing. By the time these changes are done, you will resemble a man instead of a little boy.	Like boys, your feet are often the first part of your body to start growing, followed by your arms, legs and, at the very end, your backbone. While you might feel a little disproportioned at times, don't worry. Each body part grows at its own rate, and, in a matter of time, your body will catch up with the faster-growing parts.
The first body part that starts to grow is your feet. Since they are the fastest-growing bones in your body, they end up being the appropriate size before the rest of your body can catch up. After that, your shoulders will start to grow broader, and your hips may grow a little as well, though	Another body part that starts growing is your hips. As your hipbones widen, soft, fatty tissues start growing on the hips, thighs, and buttocks. When your hips become

they will seem very narrow compared to your shoulders. Your legs and your arms will probably elongate more than your backbones, resulting in your chest looking shorter than your legs.

You will also develop muscles, especially in your arms and legs. As they develop, you will get stronger, and your chest will get bigger due to muscles and fat.

Your nipples may change as well and may get a little bigger and darker. Some of you may experience or already have experienced swelling and pain around the nipples. This is caused by hormones and will go away when the hormones lessen.

Deeper voices

Along with your body shape, your voice will also start to change after your growth spurt has begun. This usually happens around the age of

larger, your waist will look narrower in comparison, giving you a rounder, more hour-glass shape.

Breasts

Your breasts begin to grow because of a hormone called 'oestrogen', which creates tissue in the breasts. This tissue allows you to produce and store milk when you have a baby.

Your nipples and areola (the ring of skin around your nipples) are the first parts of the breast to change.

They will enlarge and become more prominent than usual, and your areola will darken. You might even see tiny bumps in the areola; these are used to protect the nipple while breastfeeding.

You may experience swelling or pain in your breasts, especially when they are bumped or hit.

Your breasts are the most

fourteen or fifteen.

Your voice becomes lower and deeper because of a hormone called testosterone. Testosterone causes the voice box (larynx) to grow larger, and, as your vocal cords get thicker and longer, your voice gets lower and deeper.

The first sign that your voice is changing is when it suddenly squeaks or cracks when you're talking. You may find this embarrassing, but this process is normal.

sensitive part of your body, and the smallest stimulation can cause pain or discomfort. In fact, they are so sensitive that cold weather or physical touch will make your nipples hard and erect.

It takes around four years for the breasts to fully develop. If your breasts start to grow unevenly, there is no need to worry. Like penises, breasts and nipples come in all shapes and sizes, which are determined by your genes and the amount of fatty tissue in the breasts.

Reflection Corner

You are fifteen, and someone comments on your chest. They say you look like a girl because it looks like you have breasts. You become self-conscious about your chest and avoid swimming lessons because you fear what your friends will say.

It is not uncommon for boys

Reflection Corner

You are fourteen years old, and you have not developed breasts yet. All of the other girls in your class have, and the boys are calling you 'pancake'. You are so embarrassed that you dread going to school every day, and you're frustrated as to why your breasts have not started developing yet.

to have swelling under their nipples. Approximately 65 per cent of boys have breast tissue during puberty, and it can be there for a number of years.

The next time someone makes a comment, or you feel self-conscious about your chest, remember that this is a part of growing into a young adult, and you are not alone.

The best way to overcome this situation is simply to ignore the teasing. Try to laugh it off or show that the teasing does not bother you. Eventually, they will get bored and leave you alone.

You may just be a late bloomer. Late bloomers are usually the ones who go through changes at a very rapid pace later than your peers. Just be patient and focus on who you as a person are rather than what you look like.

Penis

The penis is made of muscles that surround a narrow tube called the 'urethra' through which urine and semen pass. The head or the tip of the penis is the most sensitive and delicate part of the organ.

When you are born, the head of the penis is covered by a small, thin fold of skin, called the 'foreskin'. In many parts of the world, the foreskin is

Vagina

Your private parts have three distinct holes: the vagina, the urethra and the anus.

While the adult vagina is strong, stretchy and muscular, a young girl's vagina is thin and cannot stretch as much.

This is one of the reasons why childbirth is extremely dangerous for young girls because their vagina can removed during a procedure called circumcision. This is done for religious or health purposes.

Penis size varies and has nothing to do with your body size. When soft, your penis will look small in comparison to when it is fully erect.

Hanging below the penis is the scrotum, which is like a bag or sack of skin. The scrotum holds the testes' or 'testicles' where the sperm is made. During puberty, your scrotum will get looser and start to hang lower. When feeling cold, scared or sexually aroused, it will get tighter and draw up closer to your body.

Erections

When a male's penis is erect, more blood is flowing in and out of it. Because of this, the penis becomes larger and harder, and it stands out from the body. An erect penis usually curves slightly upwards, and it tear or even burst during childbirth, which can lead to serious health problems and even death.

During puberty, your vagina will begin to produce a thick, sticky fluid or discharge which comes at various times and keeps the vagina clean. It also maintains the proper environment in which 'good' bacteria can grow while also preventing infections.

Practising good hygiene

Women have to do a lot more than men when taking care of their private parts.

Here are some tips to help keep your vagina clean:

• The anus should be washed regularly and kept dry.

• Avoid sharing towels with family members or friends to prevent passing infections from one person to another.

may even curve to the side.

When your penis is erect, you cannot urinate as easily because a muscle closes off the bladder. You will have to wait until the erection goes down before you can urinate.

An erection can be caused by many things, such as excitement from a sexual thought, seeing someone you find attractive and even when the penis is touched or caressed. Erections can even happen for no reason or when you are stressed. It is also common for boys to wake up in the morning with an erection.

Erections occur during all ages, from babies to old men, and they happen all the time. You may even have one while in public, such as at a bus stop or in class. When it happens

- Cotton underwear is the best material to wear for your vagina. Nylon underwear hold in moisture and heat, which causes the growth of bacteria, a problem made worse during the warmer weather. If you can't find cotton underwear, at least try to wear ones with cotton lining.

- Whenever you urinate or defecate, you should always wipe front to back to avoid pulling germs from the anus to the vagina and urethra, which can lead to an infection.

- It is not advisable to use harsh soaps or spray perfumes or vaginal deodorant on your vagina. They may be tempting and smell amazing, but they are unnecessary and harmful. These products can change the normal fluids and irritate the skin in public, you're normally the only person who is aware of it.

It is just a myth that erections mean that you need to have sex. If you wait a few minutes, your erection will go down on its own.

Practising good hygiene

If you don't have good hygiene habits, start adopting some soon. This means you need to be diligent when cleaning yourself in the shower or bath.

It is very important to wash and clean the penis every day. You should also wash your scrotum, in between your scrotum, your thighs and in between your buttocks.

inside your vagina. Instead, clean the genital area with water. Bath soap is optional, but you should never use scented soaps.

• When cleaning the vagina, separate the outer lips to clean away secretions that collect in this area.

• Never put anything other than doctor-prescribed medicines inside your vagina.

• Your discharge will not always be the same. Sometimes, it will be clear, and, other times, it will be whitish, like egg whites. If your discharge comes heavier or thicker, changes to yellow, green, or brown or causes itching in the private parts, you may have an infection.

• Bad smelling discharge, pain, or non-menstrual bleeding in the vagina are

If you are not circumcised, you need to roll back the foreskin and gently clean this area.

all signs of infections. See your doctor if you experience any of these symptoms.

When taken care of properly, the vagina is a perfectly-balanced and self-regulating environment.

Reflection Corner

Your friend shares with you that he is getting a lot of erections, especially during class. He says that he is not thinking about anyone sexually, but he notices that it is happening more than usual.

What advice would you give to your friend?

This is a common scenario for boys, but it can feel quite embarrassing. Here are some tips you or your friends can use to handle random erections:

• Focus on something unrelated. Distraction is

Reflection Corner

Your friend shares with you that her vagina is smelling and itching. She has searched on Google, and it said that she should cover the area with yoghurt.

Do you think that she is making the right decision?

There's a lot of information available at the tips of our hands. However, it is important that whatever information you find is backed up with evidence. Go and see your the key to dealing with undesirable situations.

- Cover the private area with a book, jacket, bag or anything else available. Don't make a big scene about it.

- Remember that this is normal, and it is all part of the process of becoming a young man. It's a sign of healthy sexual functioning.

doctor, as they will advise you on what you need to do.

Ejaculation

As soon as the penis starts to grow, most boys will have their first ejaculation. This can be scary, and you might be a little worried. Please, don't be! Trust the process of your development. It is a natural change you'll experience as you navigate through your teens.

Menstruation and symptoms

When you first get your period, it is a sign that big changes have taken place. It also means that you can become pregnant with a male.

During puberty, your ovaries start to mature, and, each month, they release an egg (or ovum) due to hormones. All females are born with thousands of eggs in their ovaries, and, just like sperm,

Wet dreams

Wet dreams (also referred to as nocturnal emission) occur when boys ejaculate in their sleep, so you will probably wake up feeling damp. For many boys, the first time they ejaculate is after a wet dream.

Wet dreams can occur for various reasons. It can occur when you're dreaming about something sexual, but it also happens when the dream is not sexual.

Wet dreams will happen! And there is no way to stop yourself from having them. They are by no means an indicator that you need to have sex; they are simply a part of growing up.

they are so small that you need a microscope to see them.

As the ovaries mature, so does the uterus, and, each month, a soft lining begins to form inside of it as it prepares itself to receive a fertilised egg. If the uterus does not receive a fertilised egg, the lining breaks down and passes through the cervix and out of the vagina. This process is called menstruation.

For the first few years, your period may be irregular, and it will be hard to predict when it will come. As you get older, it will become more regular, so you'll know when to expect it.

You may get pre-period symptoms each month, and these symptoms may or may not continue during your period. Below are some symptoms you can expect and what to do if you experience them.

• Your breasts may be sore

Not all boys have them, but, if you do, just remember that they are completely normal. There's nothing to be embarrassed about.

Hair

The day will come when your facial hair will appear. It usually starts at the corner of your upper lip and spreads to the top lip. Then, it moves to the cheeks and below the bottom lip. The sides of your face and your chin are usually the last places it grows.

Not everyone grows facial hair at the same speed. If your friends have grown hair while you haven't, don't worry. This just means that you are developing hair in other places first, such as under your armpits.

or tender. Wearing a supportive bra can help keep the pain under control. You may also want to try Vitamin E oil, as this can help reduce the inflammation that causes pain and tenderness in your breasts.

· You may feel bloated. Eating less salty foods will help because you reduce the amount of water your body is storing.

· Your mood may also be affected, and you will feel all kinds of emotions in a short amount of time. This is called 'premenstrual tension' or 'PMS'.

· You might experience abdominal pain or cramps caused by the muscles of the uterus contracting as the lining is being shed. These cramps may be lessened by placing a hot water bottle on the

The area around the genitals is where the first growth of pubic hair merges. This hair is long and soft but becomes coarser as the hair begins to spread. The hair spreads to the thighs and stomach, and it is often dark.

abdomen or lower stomach, or by taking a painkiller. Exercise may help, as well.

- Some girls experience extreme pain to the point of missing school. This is usually a sign that they have heavy periods or a heavy blood flow. If you have a heavy blood flow, and your menstrual cramps are unbearable, you should seek medical attention. It is unnecessary for you to suffer this much, and the pain may be a symptom of other problems.

Understanding Your Sexuality

Although sex and sexuality are sometimes seen as taboo, they are still topics that young people discuss daily. Maybe you have seen a movie with an explicit scene, maybe something popped up on your computer, or maybe your friends introduced you to something that your parents haven't yet talked about with you. Whatever led you to be curious about these topics, having the right information can help you to have an open discussion with your parents or guardians.

In this section, we will talk about sex so that you can avoid mistakes. Your body is precious, and you need to understand why. Some young people find themselves in situations that they were not prepared for, and they end up acting on impulse. There is a time for everything in life, so go slow and take the time to get prepared before you jump headfirst into something you're not ready for.

Being Aware of your Body

Part of growing up includes developing your sexuality. Sexuality and the way in which we present it is about much more than just sex; it's about learning how to be sexually healthy. A sexually healthy person understands and knows how to control their sexual behaviours in a responsible manner, especially in social situations.

Being sexually healthy can be difficult, especially because of the misleading information you see in movies, books, music, and even from your friends and family. There are a lot of movies and books that talk about sex and love as though they are the same. In reality, they are two very different things; you can be in love without having sex and you can have sex without being in love.

While movies, books, and music are a great way to keep yourself from stressing about life, they are scripted specifically for entertainment, and they won't teach you what you need to know to have successful relationships. Knowing what's true and what's false is how you can protect yourself.

If you want a book that will help you understand how to have healthy relationships when you get older, you have come to the right place. It is always important that you make sure you always stay true to yourself when you are making choices.

As you grow older, you can start being sexually healthy in different ways, such as:

Staying informed as much as possible, knowing the difference between myth and fact and understanding the consequences of unprotected sex.

Taking the time to learn about your body and emotions, what you like or dislike and how to be safe.

Learning which choices are safe and comfortable for you, and learning to say 'no' or 'not yet' to choices you do not like.

Learning and knowing how to best protect yourself.

Making Your Own Choices

As you get older, you might start to be pressured into doing things that you wouldn't want to do otherwise. Boys may be pressured into having sex to feel like a man. Your friends might be teasing you that you haven't had sex yet, and you might be getting more attention from women. Girls might be pressured into having sex to feel beautiful. Before, your family were the only people to make you feel good about yourself; now, you might be getting attention from random boys and even older men.

IF YOU'RE DOING something that you don't want to do simply because you're being pressured into it, you should not be doing it. However, if you do decide to have sex, it is important to take the time to reflect on why. Why are you having sex? Why with this person? Why now? Is this something you need to do? What will you gain from this? You should never rely on the voice of others to determine who you really are.

SOME YOUNG PEOPLE don't have the necessary information to make good choices, and they end up making decisions they later regret. Having the right information is key to making smart decisions, and the information on the following pages will help you become informed thinkers as you navigate through adolescence toward adulthood. The aim here is to provide information that supports your decisions as you start living your best life. So, sit tight and let's work together to answer some of the burning questions you may have.

Let's look at a scenario of Kojo and Anna. They meet at university, and they believe they are in love and ready to have sex. Anna recalls reading a book about sexual health, and she asks Kojo if he knew what it meant to be sexually healthy. He says No and adds that he did not think it was important to read anything about this; as they were both in love, and that was all that mattered. Anna feels unsure of what to do.

What do you think Anna should do?

Being sexually healthy means being able to tell the difference between healthy behaviours and harmful ones, and it means taking the time to think it through before you act on your feelings.

Here is a short checklist of important questions to consider before acting on your sexual feelings:

How comfortable do you feel with the attention you are getting?

It is important to ask about intentions. In Anna's case, she needs to be sure that Kojo wants to be in a relationship rather than just wanting sex. Two big, red flags will pop up if Kojo only wants sex. The first is something called intuition. This is a feeling in her gut that something is off, and it's not a feeling that she should ignore. The second red flag is if Kojo randomly starts asking sexual questions, even when she tries to avoid them. If these red flags occur, it's likely that Kojo only wants sex. It's fine if that's what she wants, too, but there are many other people out there that would not use Anna for sex and give her the respect that she deserves.

Anna also needs to reflect if she truly wants to have sex with Kojo. Often, people mistake their emotional feelings with the desire to have sex, and act impulsively. Anna needs to take a step back and make sure that she's ready for what she's about to do. The decision has to be hers to make, and she shouldn't let Kojo pressure her into doing anything she might regret later on.

They both need to think if they will be putting themselves at risk of an unwanted pregnancy, HIV/AIDS or other STIs.

They also need to think about whether acting on their sexual feelings can cause any other problems, such as misunderstandings or miscommunications in the relationship.

Final note: if a person acts on their sexual feelings, they need to consider whether it will affect their personal beliefs. In many religions, having sex before marriage is strictly against the rules. Going against one's morals just because someone is pressuring them to do something will inevitably cause internal confusion.

I know that late adolescence is full of pressure from those around you to do things you might not be ready for. Reflecting on the real-life scenario above will help you to avoid tricky situations later on.

Sex

Sexual intercourse is another word for sex. But what is sex?

Sex is when two people act in an activity to reach a beautiful feeling of peace. In technical terms, sex is an act of physical intimacy between two people and involves using their genitals.

People have sex for many different reasons.

For some people, sex is mainly fun. This is when two people feel a physical connection toward each other rather than an emotional one. As we've mentioned before, having sex does not mean the two people are in love. This is referred to as casual sex, no-strings-attached sexual relationships, or 'friends with benefits'. These types of relationships are mainly for emotionally unavailable people who are not ready to invest their time or energy in a romantic relationship. Having casual sex has been described as being fun if both people agree on the future of the relationship, but it can be dangerous if one person starts to grow feelings for the other.

People also have sex to show their love and intimacy for one another. In these relationships, partners feel both a physical and emotional connection. When two people have a solid foundation of trust and companionship, sex can be an amazing way to demonstrate the love that both people feel. It should be noted, however, that some people try to use sex to create love. This never works out well, and it's not a good way to build a relationship. Strong relationships are built on friendship, trust,

49

and love, and these are the relationships that have the best sex.

Some people have sex for their own gain. Many people use sex to get what they want, like gifts, money or other favours. These situations can be dangerous, and a person can be taken advantage of. People having sex to get what they want does not make them feel good about themselves, and no one needs to sell their body to achieve their goals. It is much more rewarding to stay focused and work hard to achieve your dreams.

People have sex to fit in or impress their peers. You may have friends who have told you that they've already had sex. This might make you feel like you should have sex, as well, but you don't have to. Most of the people who talk about having sex are probably not being honest. Many people lie to feel cool, especially when it comes to sex. Just do whatever feels right for you. Don't rush to have sex if you don't want to. If your friends tease you, just hold your ground and ignore them. When they see that you don't care, they won't, either.

People also have sex to make a baby. Most couples, whether they're married or not, want a baby at some point in their lives, so they have sex for its original purpose – to reproduce. If you're a teenager, you shouldn't be thinking about having a baby for a while. There's plenty of time for that later. For now, enjoy growing up and discovering what the world has to offer!

Deciding not to have sex

Just as there are a lot of people who actively have sex, there are many people who have decided not to have sex. Some of the reasons for this decision are:

50

They are worried about the consequences, such as pregnancy or STIs and HIV/AIDS.

They are way too young and do not feel ready.

They do not want to let their parents down.

They feel that it goes against their values or their religion.

They would rather wait and concentrate on their studies.

They want to be sure that their boyfriend or girlfriend truly cares and loves them.

Reflection Corner #1

Remember Anna? She decided not to have sex with Kojo, as she did not feel ready. She wanted to be in a loving relationship with the prospects of getting married, and she felt that having sex with Kojo might ruin those chances.

Do you think Anna made the right decision?

Reflection Corner #2

Leo and Sandra are both 18 years old and have just started dating. They both feel as if they are ready to take their relationship to the next level by having sex with one another. Sandra is a virgin, but she feels she is ready because she knows she can trust Leo. Leo, however, has been sexually active since he was 16 years old. Sandra and Leo both have unprotected sex, and

Sandra ends up getting pregnant.

Leo and Sandra both thought nothing bad would happen to them because:

1. Leo believed that he was in full control as he had sex before and had not impregnated anyone in the past.

2. They both thought that, since Sandra was a virgin, she would not get pregnant.

3. They only had sex for three minutes.

The truth is that these three assumptions are the sole reasons as to why Sandra became pregnant in the first place. Pregnancy can happen the first time you have unprotected sex. For a couple that has unprotected sex, there is a one in twelve chances of pregnancy.

What are your thoughts about this situation?

Reflection Corner #3

Ruth tells Ama that she is being pressured by her boyfriend to take a picture of her breasts and send it to him. He tells her that he loves her so much and having these pictures will help their relationship become stronger. Ama tells Ruth that she should not send any nudity pictures to him. Ruth and Ama get into a huge argument, with Ruth telling Ama that she was being judgmental and was jealous because she did not have a boyfriend.

What advice would you give to Ruth and Ama?

Pornography

Pornography is sexual media content. With internet access, it is easier for teenagers to access porn sites. Most teenagers see online pornography at some stage, either by accident or on purpose.

They might also be exposed to magazines full of nudity and sex that teenagers have taken from their older siblings or fathers and bring to school.

It has been estimated that 60 per cent of 10 to 11-year-olds have smartphones. It should not be surprising that some of them will encounter porn online whether they're looking for it or not. A recent study conducted by Middlesex University found that about 53 per cent of 11 to 16-year-olds had seen explicit material online, nearly all of whom (94 per cent) had seen it by the age of 14.

There are a lot of reasons why people watch porn. Some watch porn to masturbate. Some watch porn to feed their curiosity about sex. On the whole, pornography sends negative messages about sex and relationships. It creates an altered view of consent and lacks any form of education about safe sex. Some of the acts could even be considered violent, and most of them lack any form of loving relationships. Because of this, it makes it difficult for teenagers to associate sex with love, creating a stunted ability in forming loving relationships when they get older.

When a person becomes addicted to porn, it interferes with their everyday life and affects the people around them.

Here are some signs that a person is addicted to porn:

1. They're **antisocial**: every time their family or friends invite them to gatherings, they'd rather keep to themselves. They make excuses to avoid social interactions, or they find reasons to get home as soon as possible. They may also watch porn as soon as they get home.

2. They **keep watching porn in secret**: most people keep their sexual fantasies and habits a secret. With porn addicts, they will go the extra mile to hide the fact that they watch porn more than others.

3. They **lose track of time**: they look at their clock and four hours have passed, and they have absolutely no idea where the time has gone.

Like masturbation, many people believe that watching porn is wrong due to their religious beliefs. Many of those people think it is repulsive and should be banned from the internet.

Children and teenagers mostly see pornography online, as fast internet connections and smartphones make for quick and easy access. It is important to be aware of your country's laws concerning the content of pornography, which should be upheld and respected.

Masturbation

Masturbation is the act of touching your own sexual organs, including your breasts, penis, vagina or any other body part that is sensitive to sensual stimulation.

It is generally believed that boys tend to masturbate more than girls. Some start when they hit puberty, and others start when they become adults.

While masturbation is totally normal, some people never masturbate because they feel that acting on their sexual feelings in any way will create a conflict between their religious or moral beliefs.

There are a lot of myths about masturbation that terrify people, such as:

Masturbation makes you go insane.

Masturbating makes you grow hair in weird places, like the palms of your hands.

Masturbation causes pimples.

Masturbation makes you go blind.

Masturbating makes you pale.

Masturbation uses up sperm, or it makes it impossible for a man to father children.

Masturbation makes you weak.

Masturbation causes you to lose your desire for sex.

Masturbation makes you become a proud and self-centred person.

None of these statements is true. There is no scientific evidence that masturbation causes any physical or psychological harm.

From a medical point of view, masturbation is considered a normal part of development. However, it is also normal if you do not masturbate.

Masturbation is considered a problem when:

It is excessive to the point that the person cannot function or it interferes with their daily tasks.

It is done in public places where other people may see it.

All in all, it is important to take care of yourself. Be mindful of what you are doing to your body, make informed decisions and never stop asking yourself 'Why am I doing this?' If you feel at ease and it is not causing you or anyone else harm, you are being mindful of your actions.

CLINIC

Taking Care of Your Health

Y̶ou only get one body, and you must treat it like a temple. Along with eating right and exercising, you must protect your body from harmful infections and diseases that may cause health problems, including reproductive issues.

Reproductive health problems mostly come from sexually transmitted infections or HIV/AIDS. These are extremely serious problems, and it is important to educate yourself on them.

Sexually Transmitted Infections: FAQs

What are sexually transmitted infections (STIs)?

S̶exually transmitted infections (STIs) - also known as sexually transmitted diseases (STDs) - are infections that are spread from one person to another through sexual contact. These diseases include chlamydia, gonorrhoea, genital herpes, human papillomavirus (HPV), syphilis, and HIV. Once contracted, these STIs can cause open sores, bumps or blisters, but some do not display symptoms for a long time. So imagine if Leo gave Sandra an STI such as chlamydia. What is problematic is that she was only focusing on the physical aspect of getting pregnant. Many people with chlamydia may not have any symptoms, and it can take a number of months or until the infection spreads to other parts of the body before a person becomes aware they have this STI.

How are STIs spread?

STIs are spread through contact between two people's bodily fluids (semen, vaginal fluids and blood) and through contact with infected skin. This means that a person is not only infected through sexual intercourse to get an STI – STIs like herpes or HPV (Human papillomavirus) are spread from skin-to-skin contact.

STIs can be spread from men to women, women to men and between two people of the same sex.

HIV is a potentially deadly virus known to destroy the body's ability to fight infection. Some people who have HIV may not feel sick for some time, but they are still infected with the virus. If early diagnosis is given and a person is treated, the person lowers their risk of developing many life-threatening diseases.

Other STIs, like syphilis, chlamydia, and gonorrhoea, are also very serious. They are curable and manageable, but they can have serious long-term effects. They can make boys infertile and girls unable to have babies, and they can even make it easier to contract HIV.

How common are STIs?

STIs are common, and they can infect sexually active males and females of all ages, regardless of their background or social status. The age group that seems to be affected the most are those under the age of 24. You may wonder why they are such a high risk!

Young people are at greater risk of getting an STI for several reasons.

- Young women's bodies are biologically more prone to STIs.

- Some young people do not get the recommended STD tests.

- Many young people are hesitant or embarrassed to talk openly and honestly with a doctor, nurse or parent about their sex lives.

- Not having the money, insurance or transportation can make it difficult for young people to get access to STI testing.

- Some young people have more than one sex partner.

There are about 20 million new cases of STIs each year in the United States, and about half are people between the ages of fifteen and twenty-four.

According to www.avert.org, Sub-Saharan Africa has the most serious HIV/AIDS epidemic, accounting for 71 per cent (24.7 million people) of the total global number of cases.

Reflection Corner #1

Isabel and Eric are 17. Eric had dated a few girls before meeting Isabel, but she had never dated anyone before him. He is immediately attracted to her, but Isabel has reservations. She puts them aside, however, because of her desire to be in a relationship and feel loved.

They start dating and become sexually involved after a few

weeks. A week later, Eric tells Isabel that he is not interested in continuing the relationship, as he wanted to concentrate on his studies. Isabel is devastated, and she feels unclean. She decides to get herself tested, and, to her shock, she finds out that she has an STI.

What should Isabel and Eric have done to protect themselves?

The best way to protect oneself from STIs is to not engage in sexual intercourse or to stay abstinent. That means not having any vaginal, anal, or oral sex. Remember, it is okay to say no.

Before having sex, Isabel and Eric should have been tested for any STIs, including HIV. They also should have used a condom, not only to prevent STIs but also to prevent any unwanted pregnancies.

Furthermore, Isabel and Eric should have discussed the status of their relationship beforehand, outlining the question of remaining faithful to each other.

Before having sex, Isabel and Eric needed to be ready to protect their bodies and their futures, including discussing how they would prevent STIs and pregnancy. This might seem like a lot of talking, but communication is the first step to any successful relationship, and it needs to be transparent and clear from the outset.

Isabel should also note that she has the right to set her own limits. She is allowed to say no, and Eric must respect that.

Having unprotected sex or engaging in sexual contact with someone infected with an STI can transmit the disease. Teenagers contract sexually transmitted diseases more than any other age group. Why do you think this is?

Isabel reflected and wondered how she would know if she has STI.

Anyone can get an STI from someone who doesn't show any symptoms because many STIs don't cause noticeable symptoms right away. For example, there are no signs to tell that someone has HIV at first. The only way to be sure is to get an STI test.

Some symptoms can come and ago. For example, if a sore or a rash on a person's private parts go away on its own, that person should still get tested. Even if the symptoms of an STI disappear, the infection can still be there, and it won't cure itself.

Another way Isabel and Eric could have become aware that they have an STI is to be aware of how their genitals normally look. If they know what they look like when they're healthy, they will be able to notice a problem more quickly when it happens. Syphilis, for example, causes a painless sore and is not noticeable unless a person looks closely using a mirror to observe the private parts better.

Girls should be familiar with the appearance and smell of their normal vaginal discharge. A normal vaginal discharge:

- Is like egg white – it's clear and whitish.

- Smells neutral, or, at least, not bad.

- Is not itchy.

What are the signs and symptoms of STIs?

Like stated before, some STIs have no obvious signs, especially for women. Other STIs have very noticeable symptoms.

Signs of STIs in men include:

- A wound, sore, ulcer, rash or blister on or around the penis.

- A discharge, like pus, from the penis.

- Pain or a burning feeling when passing urine.

- Pain during sexual intercourse.

- Pain and swelling of testicles.

- Abnormal swelling or growth on the genitals.

Signs of STIs in women include:

- Vaginal discharge that is thick, itchy or has a funny smell or colour.

- Pain in the lower abdomen.

- Pain or a burning feeling when passing urine.

- Pain during sexual intercourse.

- Abnormal or irregular bleeding from the vagina.

- Itching in the genital area.

Isabel thought it was impossible for her to get an STI because it was her first sexual experience. This is a mistake that many people make. The truth is that anyone having unprotected sex, regardless of their age or sexual history, runs the risk of getting an STI. Why is this?

Other Reproductive Health Problems

Not every problem in a person's private parts will be an STI. Even if a person is a virgin, they can still get several infections in their private parts, such as an infection of the urinary tract, which causes irritation or pain when they urinate. If they notice a strange discharge, pain and/or bleeding when they urinate, it is important they visit a health clinic.

Here is a list of some other reproductive health problems:

Candidiasis (yeast infections)

This is a common problem amongst girls and women, but boys can get it under their foreskin.

Candidiasis is caused by a yeast-like fungus called Candida albicans, one of the organisms that live naturally on the surface of the body. It does not usually cause problems and is held in check by the immune system and other bacteria that live in the vagina. However, if the immune system is stressed, it becomes less effective than normal, and the candida organism will multiply. This happens just before and after menstrual periods, as well as during pregnancy.

The symptoms include:

- Itchy private parts.

- Strange discharge from the vagina or from the foreskin that looks like spoilt milk.

- Swelling.

- Reddening of the skin of the vagina and labia or penis head.

This infection can be transmitted through sex with a person who has too much candida, but it is not an STI. Virgins and people who are not sexually active can get it by having too much warmth and moisture around the private parts. Tight, unbreathable underwear or tight pants during warm weather can trigger the infection.

Other factors can trigger candidiasis, such as stress and antibiotics, and people with diabetes or HIV frequently get candidiasis.

To avoid developing this infection, gently wash your private areas twice a day, avoid rubbing or scratching your genital areas, and wear clean, dry, cotton panties.

Seek proper treatment if you notice any symptoms. It can usually be cured with an anti-fungal cream or a tablet taken orally or inserted into the vagina. If a person is sexually active and shows symptoms for candidiasis, their partner should get treated as well.

If a person has repeated attacks of candidiasis, they should go to a clinic for further testing to rule out STI's

Urinary tract infections (UTIs)

This infection occurs in both men and women, but it is more common for women because it is easier for bacteria to get into their urinary tracts.

Symptoms include:

- Frequent urination.

- Pain or burning when urinating.

- Blood in the urine.

These infections can be avoided by practising good hygiene. Always clean your private parts from front to back! If you do the opposite, you may be spreading bacteria from the anus to the urinary opening.

You can also avoid a UTI by drinking plenty of fluids, urinating whenever you feel the need to and wearing cotton panties and loose clothes to keep the private parts dry.

If you suspect that you have a UTI, drink plenty of water and go to a clinic for treatment.

Cancer of the cervix

Cervical cancer is usually developed by women of forty years of age and up, but it is increasingly being seen in younger women.

Cervical cancer is easily curable if detected early in a procedure called a Pap smear. This is when some cells from your cervix (the

entrance of the womb) are observed underneath a microscope to see if any abnormal cells are likely to become cancerous. When a female is sexually active, Doctors recommend that they have a Pap smear test every three to five years.

If an unpleasant smell or discharge is coming from your vagina or you bleed during sex, please seek a doctor as these could be signs that something is wrong with your cervix.

According to the American Cancer Society, women who have had their first full-term pregnancy before the age of 17 are almost two times more likely to get cervical cancer later in life than women who waited to get pregnant until they were 25 years or older.

HIV (Human Immunodeficiency Virus) is a virus that leads to AIDS (Acquired Immune Deficiency Syndrome), which is a disease in which the body's immune system gets destroyed over the years.

When HIV enters the body, it attacks the immune system, which normally protects the body from infections. Over time, a person infected with HIV becomes unable to fight off infections and even common illnesses that otherwise would not be serious. Once the body can no longer fight off these illnesses, the person has developed AIDS.

There is absolutely no vaccine for preventing HIV infection, and there is no cure for AIDS once it has been contracted.

It takes a long time to notice the signs of this virus. A person who is infected with HIV might be healthy for years and not know that they have the virus. During that time, they could spread the virus to others without even realizing it.

On average, it takes five to ten years before there are any signs of infection with HIV, but the time it takes for someone to notice the signs of the virus depends on how strong a person's immune system is, as well as the severity of the virus. There are different strains of HIV, and some make people sick faster than others.

Because the virus attacks the immune system and makes the person more vulnerable to infections, the symptoms vary greatly depending on what infection or illness the person develops.

Some of the typical symptoms that occur are:

- Swollen lymph glands.
- Tuberculosis (TB).
- Severe weight loss and fatigue.
- Sweating, especially at night.
- Recurrent fever.
- Severe and persistent diarrhoea.
- Nausea and vomiting.
- Persistent cough.
- Skin rashes and sores in the mouth.

Although there is no cure for HIV/AIDS, there are some medications that help people live with HIV for many years without becoming ill. Unfortunately, these medications are not easily accessible to everyone, as they are extremely expensive and not available in all countries.

Between 2005 and 2016, the number of adolescents living with HIV rose by 30 per cent. According to the World Health Organization (WHO), HIV is the second leading cause of death among adolescents worldwide.

Reflection Corner

Why are adolescents vulnerable to HIV?

The best ways to avoid contracting HIV/AIDS are:

Never decide someone is 'safe' from how they look.

If a person engages in sex, they should always use protection, such as a condom. Research shows that if protection is used correctly and consistently, condoms can protect a person from HIV and other STIs.

In the case of Eric and Isabel, they should have had a test for HIV and other STIs before starting a sexual relationship.

Do not share razors, needles, piercing equipment or ceremonial knives. Sharing needles or syringes can put a person at a high risk of HIV and other infectious diseases such as hepatitis.

How does HIV enter the body?

HIV is mainly spread like any other STI: through sexual intercourse and direct contact with bodily fluids.

HIV can be spread in other ways, too:

From mother to child during pregnancy, delivery or through breastfeeding.

Through contact with the blood of an infected person. This could be through a blood transfusion, a cut with a shared

■ knife, or when drug users share needles.

■ Traditional ceremonies, like circumcision, that use unsafe practices, such as sharing one knife or razor blade among all the candidates.

■ Sharing razor blades with relatives and friends.

There is no proof that HIV can be contracted through kissing. However, if a person has a cut in their mouth, they could get HIV from kissing an infected person who also has a cut or a sore. HIV can be in semen and vaginal fluids, and if a person with a cut in their mouth gets semen or vaginal fluids in their mouth, they are prone to getting HIV.

HIV cannot be spread through casual body contact, such as hugging, shaking hands, or touching an infected person because the virus dies immediately when it gets in contact with air. It also cannot be contracted by sharing objects with an infected person, such as dishes, eating utensils, clothes, or books.

How to detect HIV?

It is difficult to tell if someone has HIV/AIDS just from looking at their body. Most of the illnesses that are associated with AIDS can come even if a person doesn't have HIV/AIDS. For example, they can have tuberculosis and never be infected with HIV/AIDS. HIV simply makes it easier to contract illnesses.

The only way to be sure that someone has HIV is if they are tested for it. In most countries, HIV testing is accompanied by a trained and sympathetic counsellor who provides in-depth discussions on how to deal with HIV status and how to properly take care of themselves.

Can a person live positively with HIV?

Although it won't be easy, many people with the virus learn how to cope with it. Not only will they need a lot of counselling, but they should also tell someone close to them so that they don't carry that heavy burden alone.

For many people, the disease will progress very slowly, and they can live with the virus for 10 to 20 years.

It is very important for a person to keep a positive outlook if they are HIV-positive. Scientists are working on finding a cure for HIV, and a breakthrough could happen at any time.

Living with HIV in a positive way greatly improves a person's chances of staying healthy for a long time. Living positively means:

- Cherishing their loved ones and spending time with their family.

- Being thankful that they are living another day.

- Getting in touch with their spirituality.

- Eating healthy foods that boost their immune system, such as greens, beans and fish.

- Treating all illnesses responsibly when they arise.

- Getting plenty of rest.

- Exercising moderately.

Consent

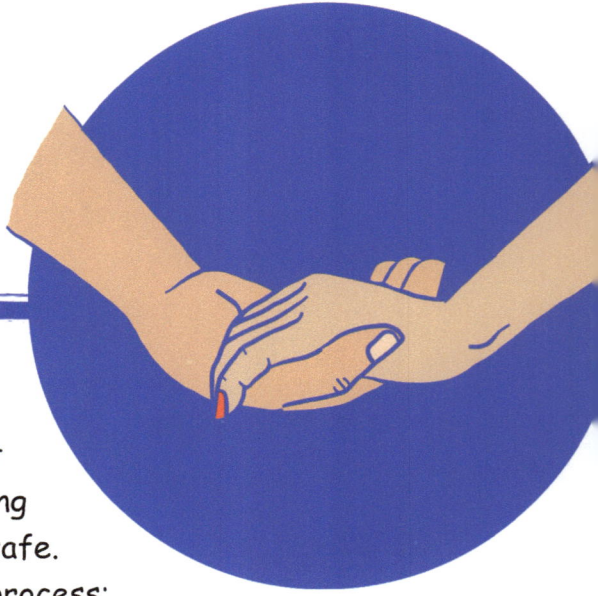

This is an important aspect of staying healthy and safe. Consent is an ongoing process; every time a person engages in sexual activity, they have to make sure that everyone involved consents, regardless of whether or not they have already been sexually active with that person. Just because they consented yesterday doesn't mean that they will consent today.

Reflection Corner

Alex and Charlie have been good friends for a long time. At the end of the school year, they went to prom together, and Alex invited Charlie to go home with him. They were both drinking quite a lot, and they ended up engaging in sexual activity. In the morning, Charlie reported that Alex had abused his power and that no consent had been sought before the sexual activity.

There are a few things that you need to know regarding consent.

A person has the right to change their mind at any point in time.

Giving and getting consent is not awkward. Consent should be treated as a form of communication.

Any sexual contact without consent is wrong and illegal, regardless of the age of the people involved.

The person consenting must agree by choice, not force!

Everyone should have the freedom and capacity to make their own decision about what they want to do and how far they want to go.

If a person is unsure about whether or not they have someone's consent, they should ask them bluntly. This eliminates any confusion or uncertainty and ensures that everyone involved is comfortable with what is happening.

Sometimes, signals such as body language or even the way a person is talking may be misinterpreted as consent. As with all communication, everything needs to be clearly addressed and understood.

Conclusion

Y ou have come to the end of the book. I hope you enjoyed it and found it useful!

These basic life skills we discussed (body changes, making your own choices, STIs, pornography and consent) are the keys to developing a healthy relationship with your body. If you master them, you will be able to not only stay safe but also love, respect, and cherish yourself.

Take a moment to reflect on where you were at the beginning of this book, how you felt during the reading process and what you have learned that you didn't know before.

Here's a fun quiz that will help you evaluate whether you might need to go back and reflect on some sections of this book a little longer.

Quiz

1. What is puberty?

2. True or false: most teenagers have some confusion or hang-ups about their bodies.

3. Growth hormones are when your …….. releases the …….. that tell your body to grow.

4. What is the newly grown hair on your private parts called?

5. True or false: some girls may start to develop breasts around age 8, but other girls start later.

6. Women have four options when caring for their periods. What are they?

7. True or false: the penis is made of muscles that surround a narrow tube called the 'urethra' through which urine and semen pass.

8. What is sex?

9. Why do people masturbate?

10. What does consent mean?

11. What is HIV?

12. What are STIs ?

13. What is the most common STI among adolescents?

14. True or false: STIs are common, and they can infect sexually active males and females of all ages, regardless of their background or social status.

15. What causes candidiasis?

16. Identify at least four ways through which HIV can be spread.

17. Why does pornography send negative messages about relationships?

18. True or false: cervical cancer is easily curable if detected early in a procedure called a Pap smear.

19. List five tips that can help you build your confidence.

20. What is identity?

How did the quiz go? Are you at a different place from where you started? Or are you still confused about some of the things we covered in this book? Remember: you can always go back and read a section again any time you need some guidance!

Well done for reaching the end of this book! I wish you the very best as you continue to embark on the journey of self-discovery – a priceless experience that we should all embrace.

Enjoy being happy; you deserve it!

More books by Dr Funke

Improve Your Thinking: A 10 Step Guide

Love your Authentic Self: A 10 Step Guide

Take Control of Your Tomorrow

Good Monday Morning

High Risk Body Size

Notes

About the Author

Dr. Funke Baffour-Awuah, better known as '**Dr. Funke**', is a renowned psychologist, and published author. She works with children, adults and families helping with a wide range of modern day issues.

Dr Funke's goal in life is to be the best version of herself and she strives to empower others to also do the same. She is passionate and driven in all that she does, focused on helping people to help themselves.

Dr. Funke has created her own educational wellbeing programmes based on this notion and assists people to develop key strategies that empower and develop them.

Currently, **Dr Funke** is in Ghana working with young people and has been involved in developing policies and procedures concerning child protection and special educational needs.

Dr Funke is also embracing an educational tour focusing on an'Improving your thinking programme'. Her vision is to support schools to engage in the programme that promotes emotional wellbeing among young people. Aside from her professional roles, she spends her time illustrating comic characters and uses her illustrations as part of her practice.

www.ingramcontent.com/pod-product-compliance
Lightning Source LLC
Chambersburg PA
CBHW042004100426
42737CB00040BA/107